# LIFE IN THE ANTARCTIC

## ANTARCTICA

Lynn M. Stone

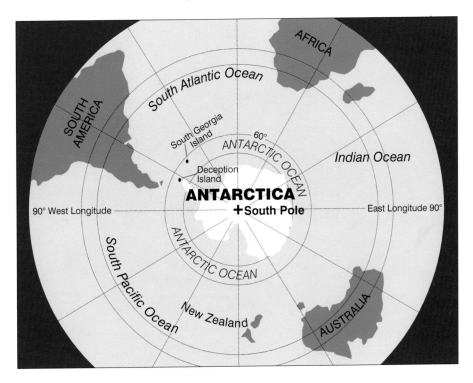

The Rourke Book Co., Inc.
Vero Beach, Florida 32964

PHOTO CREDITS
All photos © Lynn M. Stone except p. 10 © Doug Cheeseman

**Library of Congress Cataloging-in-Publication Data**

Stone, Lynn M.
   Life in Antarctica / by Lynn M. Stone.
      p.  cm. — (Antarctica)
   Includes index.
   ISBN 1-55916-143-4
   1. Ecology—Antarctica—Juvenile literature.   2. Food chains
(Ecology)—Antarctica—Juvenile literature.   [1. Ecology—Antarctica ]
I. Title  II. Series: Stone, Lynn M.   Antarctica.
QH84.2.S86  1995
574.5' 0998' 9—dc20                                        95–6893
                                                                    CIP
                                                                     AC

**Printed in the USA**

# TABLE OF CONTENTS

# LIFE IN THE ANTARCTIC

Antarctica is the great white, frozen island continent. A layer of ice and frosting of snow cover almost all of Antarctica.

Few plants or animals can live on icy Antarctica. However, life is plentiful in the sea and on some of the islands around Antarctica.

Millions of seabirds live in the Antarctic neighborhood. Millions of seals live in the region, too, along with thousands of great whales.

*King penguins crowd together on an island colony in the Antarctic region*

# CHAINS OF LIFE

All animals must eat to survive. Food gives them the energy they need.

Food energy moves from one living thing to another. In doing so, it links Antarctic plants and animals together in a series of food chains.

The biggest, strongest animals are said to be at the top of the food chain. A seal, for example, is near the top of food chains. The seal may get food energy from eating a fish. But from what did the fish get its energy?

*The southern elephant seal of the Antarctic feeds largely on fish*

# LIFE IN THE ICE

The fish eaten by the seal lived by eating other, smaller creatures. The fish borrowed energy from them. What had they lived on?

Almost all Antarctic food chains begin with a simple plant called **algae** (AL gee). Algae can grow where bigger, rooted plants cannot. It even grows between Antarctic sea ice and snow!

Algae themselves grow by changing sunlight—solar energy—into food. When spring melts the snow, the algae is released into the Antarctic Ocean.

*Spring break-up of Antarctica's ice pack releases tiny plants into the sea*

# LIFE IN THE SEA

The algae becomes part of a huge floating "stew" of tiny plants and animals known as **plankton** (PLANK ton). Many of the larger plankton animals eat smaller plankton animals. They, in turn, are food for fish, squid, seals and whales.

One of the larger forms of plankton is krill. Krill is a close cousin of shrimp. Great swarms of the two and one half inch long krill swim in the Antarctic Ocean.

*Shrimplike krill in the Antarctic plankton stew are a major source of food for larger animals*

11

*Antarctic petrels searching for fish or krill flit over the ocean*

*Elephant seals and penguins share Antarctic shores and seas together*

## KRILL

Krill are extremely important to life in the Antarctic. They are a major source of food for certain kinds of penguins, seals, whales and fish.

The huge blue, fin, sei and minke whales travel into Antarctic seas each spring to fatten up on krill. These huge animals filter krill from the sea through a series of mouth plates called **baleen** (bay LEEN).

*A great humpback whale hunts for krill in the Antarctic Ocean*

## PLANTS

One way or another, Antarctic animals depend upon the sea for their food. Antarctic land has few plants, so it produces very little food.

On ice-covered Antarctica itself, plants have almost no open ground on which to grow. The dry, cold air and harsh winds limit plant growth, too.

Except for two small flowering plants, the Antarctic continent has only mosses, algae and **lichens** (LIE kins).

*Antarctic mosses grow among rocks that are colored by lichen*

# PREDATORS

Animals that attack and kill other animals for their **prey** (PRAY), or food, are **predators** (PRED uh tors). The largest predators may feed on smaller predators. Killer whales eat seals that prey on the fish that eat smaller fish.

Antarctic predators, whether seals, fish, whales or seabirds, hunt in the ocean. Most of the big Antarctic predators spend part of their lives on shore. They depend upon the ocean for their prey, however. Even penguins, which may remain ashore for months, feed only at sea.

*Penguins rest and nest ashore, but feed at sea with other Antarctic predators*

## SCAVENGERS

**Scavengers** (SKA ven jers) are nature's clean-up crew. They eat leftovers. When animals die on Antarctic shores, they are not wasted. Scavengers gobble them up.

Most scavengers are too small to see. However, three Antarctic birds—the sheathbill, giant petrel and skua—scavenge in full view!

These birds have "jobs" in the community similar to the jobs of vultures and crows in warmer lands.

*The pigeonlike sheathbill, always on the lookout for food, patrols a chinstrap penguin colony*

# THE CHANGING LIFE OF THE ANTARCTIC

Life in the Antarctic region has changed in the last 100 years. For example, the great whales were nearly wiped out by hunting. Even with protection, they have been slow to come back.

Without as many whales to eat them, krill have increased. Krill-eating penguins and seals have increased, also.

The possibility that the Earth is slowly warming may further change life in the Antarctic.

# Glossary

**algae** (AL gee) — a group of rootless, nonflowering plants that can live in conditions where many other plants cannot

**baleen** (bay LEEN) — the mouth plates which filter food from the sea for certain large whales

**lichen** (LIE kin) — plantlike growths that are combinations of algae and fungi

**plankton** (PLANK ton) — tiny, floating plants and animals of the seas and other bodies of water

**predator** (PRED uh tor) — an animal that kills other animals for food

**prey** (PRAY) — an animal that is hunted for food by another animal

**scavenger** (SKA ven jer) — an animal that feeds on dead animals and leftovers

# INDEX